The Norwich Gates

Sandringham Woods

To Dersingham

5

Admiral's Drive

To Sandringham Estate Woodyard

Wild Fallow Deer Stag

Old Father Time Statue

North Garden

Bleached Lime Avenue

Land Train Stop

2

To Persimmon Statue 300 yds

The Museum Belltower

West Lawns

WC

4

3

B1440

Stream Walk

York Cottage

York Cottage (Private)

CONTENTS

Map of Grounds . . . . .front inside cover

Introduction 3

The Grounds 6

The House 10

The Saloon 12

The Corridor 16

The Small Drawing Room 17

The Drawing Room 20

The Dining Room 26

The Lobby 29

Ballroom Corridor 30

The Ballroom 32

A Royal Watercolour 34

The Museum 36

The Church 42

Sandringham and the Visitor 43

Wildlife Sketchbook 44

Sandringham in Winter 46

The Estate and Royal Stud 48

Royal Family Tree . . . . . . .back inside cover

*A detail of
The Norwich
Gates*

The old main entrance and drive came straight to the House through the Norwich Gates. The gates are a masterpiece of Victorian craftsmanship. This enormous and elaborate structure in wrought and cast iron was a wedding gift to Prince Edward and Princess Alexandra from the county of Norfolk and the city of Norwich. Designed by Thomas Jekyll and made by Barnard Bishop and Barnard of Norwich, the gates won a prize at the 1862 International Exhibition. The central shield in the overthrow has on one side the Royal Arms encircled by the Garter and on the other the Prince of Wales' feathers. The seated gryphons on top of the gate piers carry shields painted with the Arms of the Duchy of Cornwall and the Earldom of Chester.

INTRODUCTION AND SHORT HISTORY

BY HIS ROYAL HIGHNESS
THE DUKE OF EDINBURGH

In the spring of 1862, Sandringham House with its estate of 7,000 acres was bought from the Hon Charles Spencer Cowper as a country home for Albert Edward, Prince of Wales who had just turned twenty one. Prince Edward, the eldest son of Queen Victoria and the Prince Consort, was later to succeed his mother as King Edward VII. His father had died the previous year, but not before he had made arrangements to provide £220,000 to purchase the property and a further £60,000 for improvements.

It so happens that Charles Spencer Cowper was the stepson of Viscount Palmerston who was Prime Minister at the time and who lived at Broadlands in Hampshire. Broadlands was later inherited by Edwina, Countess of Mountbatten and became the home of Admiral of the Fleet, The Earl Mountbatten of Burma and their family.

After King Edward VII's death, one of his friends wrote: "Up to the last year of his life he was continually improving his domain, repairing churches, spending money on the place in one way or another". His son, King George V, wrote: "Dear old Sandringham, the place I love better than anywhere else in the world".

On his death at Sandringham in 1936, the Estate was inherited by King Edward VIII who sold it after his abdication to his brother, King George VI, whose affection for it was no less keen: "I have always been happy here," he wrote to his mother, "and I love the place". He died at Sandringham in February 1952 when the Estate passed to his elder daughter.

Albert Edward, Prince of Wales and Alexandra, Princess of Wales in a carriage by the main entrance, Sandringham Hall 1863

A J Humbert's early idea for the new Sandringham House

It is only too evident from the amount of time that the present Queen and her family spend here that this affection continues as strongly as ever.

The gardens were first opened to the public by King Edward VII in 1908 and in 1930 the museum, created by King George V, was opened with an admission charge of three pence. It was the wish of the present owner for the House itself to be opened to the public in 1977.

Sandringham has remained the private country home of four generations of sovereigns: Prince Edward's son, King George V; his grandson King George VI; and, his great grand-daughter, the present Queen, Elizabeth II.

Sandringham is recorded in the Domesday Book of 1086 as "Sant Dersingham", the sandy part of Dersingham, subsequently shortened to Sandringham. There is evidence of a residence on the present site of the House as early as 1296, although prehistoric flint implements have been found in the vicinity and there are remains of a Roman villa quite close to nearby Appleton Farm.

The old hall at Sandringham, 1862

In a 1901 signed photograph, King Edward VII is seen with his three successors, Kings George V, Edward VIII and George VI

Victoria Mary, Duchess of York at York Cottage, June 1895

Prince Albert Edward and Princess Alexandra, 1863

Alexandra, Princess of Wales with some of her dogs at Sandringham, June 1900

From the sixteenth century, the area passed through two families: the Cobbes who held the land from 1517 and the Hostes who followed in 1686. The house Prince Edward found at Sandringham, a plain Georgian structure with a stucco exterior, was built in the second half of the eighteenth century by Cornish Henley whose wife was a member of the Hoste family. Henley died before it was completed and his son eventually sold it to a neighbour who bequeathed it in his will to his friend Charles Spencer Cowper.

The Prince made the old house habitable and moved in with his new wife, Princess Alexandra of Denmark, three weeks after their marriage in March 1863. As their family and household grew, two new houses were built in the grounds: Bachelors' Cottage for guests and Park House for members of the household. Much later, Park House was let to Lord Fermoy, the local Member of Parliament, whose daughter Frances was born there and who later married Viscount Althorp, Earl Spencer's son. In 1955, by a strange quirk of fate, the Althorps came to live at Park House where their children were born. Their youngest daughter, Lady Diana Spencer, was later to marry His Royal Highness The Prince of Wales. Today, Park House is let at a peppercorn rent to the Cheshire Homes Foundation as a hotel for the disabled.

It soon became evident that the old house was too cramped for the Prince's growing family. Accordingly, it was demolished to make way for a new one, designed by A J Humbert and built by Goggs Brothers of Swaffham. The House was completed in 1870, but eleven years later a ballroom, designed by R W Edis, was added on the east side to increase the capacity for entertaining.

Above from left: Prince Albert; Princess Mary; Prince Edward and Prince Henry of Wales; George, Prince of Wales

In November 1891, disaster struck when a fire broke out destroying fourteen rooms on the upper floor and much of the roof. Despite the fact that the House had only a temporary roof, the Prince insisted on spending his birthday there. The following January, the family suffered a dreadful tragedy: the Prince's eldest son, Albert Victor, Duke of Clarence caught influenza at Sandringham, pneumonia set in and he died on 14th January, just after his twenty eighth birthday.

In 1893, the Prince's second son, George, Duke of York married Princess Mary of Teck and went to live in Bachelors' Cottage which was then renamed York Cottage. With the exception of King Edward VIII, all of his children were born there and the family continued to occupy this modest house until Queen Alexandra died in 1925. York Cottage was subsequently converted to the Estate Office and flats for employees.

SILVER WEDDING
1923~1948

We are much touched to receive the beautiful Silver Wedding Present from all at Sandringham. We are most grateful not only for your share in the gift of the Silver Partridges, but also for your loyal greetings & best wishes to us on the 25th Anniversary of our Wedding Day.

A Silver Wedding 'Thank you' from King George VI and Queen Elizabeth

The traditional family gathering at Sandringham, Christmas 1951, barely two months before the death of King George VI and the succession of HM Queen Elizabeth II

THE GROUNDS

Bachelors' Wing Terrace

Stream Walk

Prince Edward and Princess Alexandra took an enthusiastic interest in the design and layout of the gardens around the House. William Broderick Thomas, a landscape gardener, was employed to advise them and a major redevelopment of the grounds was undertaken. The public road that ran close to the north end of the House was moved further away; an upper spring fed lake and a lower stream fed lake were created; and a large rockery was constructed on the east side of the upper lake. In 1913, Sir Dighton Probyn VC, Queen Alexandra's Comptroller, had a charming little summer house built in this rockery as a gift for the Queen. Flower beds and a rose garden were laid out on what is now the big lawn on the west side of the House and a great variety of trees was planted to screen it from view while allowing vistas through to the park at strategic points.

In Queen Alexandra's time the elaborate gardens and grounds were maintained by some sixty gardeners. With the death of the Queen in 1925, followed only eleven years later by that of her son, King George V, and then by six years of war, they suffered severely. However, due largely to the efforts of King George VI in the years immediately after the war, the gardens were restored and improved.

Sundial, south front, 1892: 'Let others tell of storms and showers I'll only count your sunny hours'

*The North Garden
in high summer*

*Early summer is
rhododendron time*

The King lived in rooms on the first floor at the north end of the House and it irked him that people standing at the Norwich Gates could look down the drive and watch him shaving in the morning.

Accordingly, he had a raised shrubbery bed and some Scots pine planted on the direct line between his windows and the road and diverted the drive around it.

Sir Geoffrey Jellicoe, who had helped the King with the design of the garden at Royal Lodge in Windsor Great Park, was tasked with designing a border between the north door and the shrubbery bed, the design to incorporate two double avenues of pleached limes, based on the pattern in the gardens at St Paul's Walden which belonged to the King's brother-in-law, Sir David Bowes-Lyon.

*HM The Queen
in the North
Garden*

*Memorial to 'The faithful
companion of The Queen'*

King George VI's North Garden

At the far end of this arrangement of box hedges, herbaceous flowers and roses is a large gilded figure of Kuvera, the Buddhist divinity, brought from China in 1869 by Admiral Sir Henry Keppel and given to Prince Edward. It is generally known as 'John Chinaman'.

The eighteenth century figure of Father Time on the axis of the border was a gift from Queen Mary in 1950. Sir Geoffrey also laid out the drive to the front of the House between two serrated yew hedges.

8

Retired Head Gardener Fred Waite
by the Stream Walk in spring

The Glade
Below: The North Garden

In the late 1960s, Her Majesty The Queen invited
Sir Eric Savill, Deputy Ranger of Windsor Great
Park and the famous creator of the Savill and Valley
Gardens at Windsor, to remodel the areas between
the lawns and the garden wall. The present layout
of paths and glades and the arrangement of flowers
and shrubs are his creation, as are the beds and
paths by the Jubilee Gates. Landscaping of the
stream, which comes under the wall and feeds the
lower lake in front of York Cottage, was carried out
by Fred Waite, who retired in early 1996 after 27
years as Head Gardener.

THE HOUSE

Inscription above the door of the saloon

Prince Edward and Princess Alexandra employed A J Humbert, a London architect, to design their new home. Fronted in red brick and dressed with sandstone, the neo-Jacobean style House has a gabled roof and picturesque turrets. Of the old hall, only the conservatory was retained for conversion to a billiard room. Overlooking the west terrace, it is constructed of red-brown local carrstone, the same material used to add a bowling alley, now converted to a library. In 1891 the Bachelors' Wing was built above it.

New furniture, much of it from the London firm of Holland and Sons, was commissioned for the new house which was decorated in the latest style, as befitted the home of a young prince and princess at the centre of fashionable society. Guests from all over the world were entertained here but Queen Victoria visited only twice, describing the House as "handsome".

In 1888 Prince Edward wrote to Charles Carrington, his lifelong friend, "I have, I think, finished all my improvements here . . . and I think I have every reason to be satisfied". Carrington agreed. He described Sandringham later as "the most comfortable house in England".

The east front of Sandringham with the A J Humbert porte-cochère and entrance door

A J Humbert's sketch of the chosen design for Sandringham House

The Prince and Princess of Wales, Prince
Albert Victor and Princess Maud with detail
left of the newly built Sandringham House
painted by Heinrich von Angeli

THE SALOON

Entering the House under the impressive porte-cochère, stone steps rise to an oak door behind which delicately etched glass panelled doors lead into the saloon. Within a few paces, guests and visitors are welcomed into the heart of the House.

Inside, above the door, is a painted inscription: "This house was built by Albert Edward Prince of Wales and Alexandra his wife in the year of Our Lord 1870".

A weighing stool, dated November 1872, stands just inside the entrance. Traditionally used by jockeys, the scales were used to weigh guests on arrival and departure: by providing rich food and fine wines, a good host in Victorian England should add at least a few ounces to the weight of each guest!

The saloon in 1901

When the Royal family are in residence the fire in the saloon is always lit. Princess Alexandra's grand piano is unusually faced with carved oak and was specially made for the saloon by John Broadwood and Sons. The nameboard is inlaid with the Prince of Wales' feathers in engraved ivory

A green baize covered table always displays a jigsaw puzzle

The largest room in Sandringham House in 1870, the saloon, in the style of a Jacobean hall, is two storeys high with a hammer beam roof and lofty windows. The minstrels' gallery is supported by columns and arches. Underneath hangs a portrait by Heinrich von Angeli of Prince Edward and Princess Alexandra with their eldest son, Prince Albert Victor, Duke of Clarence and Avondale and their youngest daughter, Princess Maud, later Queen of Norway.

14

Ambush II

Comfortable armchairs and sofas fill the saloon which is used by the Royal family as a sitting room. Originally, it was also used for balls, parties and theatrical entertainment but a decision was taken in 1881 to add a ballroom to save the disruption of frequent furniture removal. Queen Mary, an accomplished and prolific producer of fine needlework, was responsible for many of the tapestry cushions and seat covers here and throughout the House.

The three seventeenth century Brussels tapestries by Gilis D Brier depict the life of the Roman Emperor, Constantine the Great. Around the upper walls hang shields of arms which continue in stained glass in the top tier of the windows.

The original Victorian fireplaces at each end of the room were replaced in 1938 with genuine Jacobean chimney pieces; the north end fireplace still has the original dark overmantel. Constructed in carved stone, they have matching firebacks and firedogs decorated with Royal coats of arms. Above the south end fireplace stand two nineteenth century silvered wood Italian candelabra and a Swiss bracket clock. The latter, in ebonised wood with gilt bronze mounts, plays many different chimes. It is one of around one hundred and eighty clocks in Sandringham House, all of which are kept in good time.

Winterhalter portraits grace the saloon: Queen Victoria (1845) and the Prince Consort (1850)

In Edward VII's day, clocks were set half an hour early to make the most of daylight for shooting. Known as 'Sandringham time', the custom continued until 1936.

A barograph and a wind speed and direction meter stand on the elaborately veneered and inlaid table. These became, and remain, important weather indicators for planning the outdoor sporting activities which have always been so much part of life at Sandringham.

Family photographs, spanning more than a century, decorate tables and the piano. Bronze and painted wood sculptures of some of the famous horses owned by the Royal family adorn window sills and the oak side-table.

Columbus

Swiss bracket clock

THE CORRIDOR

The central corridor links the principal rooms and two main staircases of the House. Trophies of arms and armour dating from the seventeenth to the nineteenth centuries hang on the walls. Many of these were gifts presented to the Prince of Wales by maharajahs and princes on his tour of India and the Far East in 1875 and 1876. One of a pair of Chinese oval cisterns from the Ch'ien Lung dynasty stands on a Victorian oak cabinet.

Family portraits, paintings of horses and dogs and bronze sculptures can be seen through the doors at each end of the corridor.

THE SMALL DRAWING ROOM

The delicate decoration of this room is reflected in the walls which are hung with English silk, manufactured in Suffolk. Much of the porcelain is Meissen and Copenhagen acquired by Princess Alexandra in the last quarter of the nineteenth century. The decoration is floral or musical, themes which continue on the set of three Sheraton style armchairs which are painted with flowers and musical instruments. The seat covers were worked by Queen Mary in 1935.

The fine porcelain chandelier, though unmarked, is probably Dresden. A gift from the Kaiser to Prince Edward, it matches the mirror frame between the windows.

Above the veneered and gilt bronze mounted bookcases hang August Schiatt's portraits of King Christian IX and Queen Louise of Denmark, Queen Alexandra's parents. Two of her daughters, Princess Louise and Princess Victoria, appear in the painting by Bauerle. On each side of the fireplace hangs one of a pair of oil paintings by Chevilliard showing A *priest reading* and A *priest yawning*.

Christmas at Sandringham has been special since the time of King Edward VII. In 1932 King George V made the first Christmas radio broadcast live from Sandringham and in 1992 Her Majesty recorded the Christmas Day message to the Commonwealth in the small drawing room.

Copenhagen vase and cover painted with a Danish summer palace

Photograph: David Secombe/BBC Picture Archive

Recording the 1992 Christmas broadcast to the Commonwealth

Above: Mallard duck and ducklings: birds on display are gifts to HRH The Duke of Edinburgh, President of the Worldwide Fund for Nature

The Prince and Princess of Wales attended the
opening of the Vienna Exhibition in 1873. It is
said that the artist, Nicholas Chevalier, included a
portrait of his girlfriend in the crowd, her face
illuminated by soft light

Detail of
porcelain mirror

Meissen cabaret set,
late 19th century,
encrusted with blue
forget-me-nots and insects

THE DRAWING ROOM

The Royal family and their guests often gather in the drawing room where they can enjoy the afternoon and early evening light through the west facing windows. Queen Victoria described it in her journal of 1871 as "[a] very long and handsome drawing room, with painted ceilings and panels with two fireplaces . . ."

Alexandra, Princess of Wales and her daughters (left to right) Princess Victoria, Princess Louise and Princess Maud of Wales, in the drawing room, 1882

The delicate influence of Alexandra is evident in the overall décor of the main drawing room but is also present in the display cabinets. The upright showcase on the left hand side of the room contains a collection of Chinese figures from the 18th and 19th centuries depicting animals and plants in agate, amber, jade, quartz and rock crystal

Background: The trompe l'oeil
ceiling painting

The drawing room in
the 1890s

collection of figures in semi-precious stone, jade and
amber. In the early 1900s, the collection was
dominated by the works of Carl Fabergé,
patronised first by Prince Edward and Princess
Alexandra but equally popular with succeeding
generations of the Royal family.

Many of the Russian and
Scandinavian silver, silver gilt,
cloisonné and piqué-à-jour enamel
pieces now displayed here were
gifts to Princess Alexandra from
her sister Dagmar, who married
Tsar Alexander III. Worcester
porcelain in the cabinet by the bay
window was acquired by Queen
Mary and dates from the late
eighteenth century.

The division of the room
into two interconnected
spaces reflects the
arrangement in the old hall
where a drawing room was
created by knocking together
two rooms; the effect was so
much admired that it was
repeated in the new house.

Glass fronted display cabinets were
built into the walls to house the

The collection of miniatures includes
British silverware, notably the miniature silver
tea services.

One of the pair of French 19th century turquoise vases
painted in the 18th century manner of Sèvres porcelain

The bow window in the drawing room looks out upon the lawns and faces west, with the full benefit of sunlight in the afternoon

To symbolise the Royal marriage the hand painted beechwood armchairs bear the feathers of the Prince of Wales, bound by the love knot

Italian craftsmen were brought to Sandringham to carve the intricate panelling on the walls and cornices and to paint the *trompe l'oeil* ceiling panels. The golden pheasant, which Prince Edward introduced to the Estate, features on the rectangular panel while white doves flutter on the round. In the corners, oval panels are painted with musical instruments to match gilt finger panels on the doors.

Three beautiful portraits are set into the wall panelling. These charming studies in romantic style, painted by Edward Hughes in 1896, depict Princess Alexandra and her two youngest daughters. Princess Alexandra is shown holding in her right hand a delicate cameo of her late son, Albert Victor, Duke of Clarence.

The romantic style continues in the marble sculptures. Mary Thornycroft's innocent childish couple (below) and F G Villa's Cupid binding the eyes of Venus (opposite) are typical of Victorian mythological statuary.

The delightful giltwood screen contains mounted photographs of family, friends and guests of Prince Edward and Princess Alexandra. These include actors, musicians, composers and statesmen.

The elaborately gilded glazed cabinets at the south end of the room, surmounted by Meissen figurines, are probably German and contain silver gilt and Bohemian glass.

Princess Victoria (1868-1935), who remained unmarried

Princess Maud (1869-1938), whose marriage made her Queen of Norway

Queen Alexandra, when Princess of Wales,
by Edward Hughes. 'In the production of
what may be called pleasing family
likenesses he is without rival'

25

THE
DINING ROOM

The mahogany dining table has nine leaves and is capable of being extended to seat twenty two people. The Copeland Mecklenburg-Strelitz dinner service was a gift from the citizens of Norwich to the Duke and Duchess of York, later King George V and Queen Mary. It is an 1883 replica of a Chelsea porcelain service presented in 1763 by King George III and Queen Charlotte to her brother, The Duke of Mecklenburg-Strelitz. The original is in Buckingham Palace. Racehorses belonging to Her Majesty The Queen decorate the table mats and each crystal glass bears the Royal cypher, E II R.

Minton dinner and dessert services, turquoise and gold on white grounds in the Sèvres style, stand on the sideboard and side tables. The dessert service, a gift from Queen Victoria, was decorated by Henry Mitchell, a leading nineteenth century painter of porcelain, with copies of the works of Landseer who was one of Queen Victoria's favourite artists.

Menu card holder: part of a Minton dinner service given to Prince Edward and Princess Alexandra by Queen Victoria and decorated with their entwined initials

Veneered with tortoiseshell and fitted with gilt bronze mounts, the dining room clock, signed on the dial by the Danish clockmaker, Hans Hein of Helsingor

26

In 1991 the Spanish tapestries were cleaned, restored and re-hung after hanging in the Sandringham dining room for over a hundred years

The walnut and mahogany panelling was originally decorated only with touches of gilt, but the entire room was painted Braemar green in 1938 to enhance the display of magnificent Spanish tapestries which adorn the walls. A gift, in 1876, from King Alfonso XII of Spain to the Prince of Wales, the tapestries depict the work of seven Spanish artists. The work of Goya is represented by two panels: one, above the sideboard, shows a wedding procession and the other, between the windows, a man and woman walking in the country.

THE LOBBY

O ak cases line the walls of the gun lobby. These contain a rare collection of sporting shotguns, rifles and pistols owned and used by successive generations of the Royal family. The works of all of England's finest gunmakers are represented.

Amongst the family sketches and watercolours in the lobby is a painting by John Gilbert showing Queen Victoria, Prince Albert and their family meeting wounded Coldstream Guards, returned from the Crimea, in the grand hall at Buckingham Palace in 1856. On a lighter note, the series of witty sketches by Rien Poortvliet captures vividly the essence of a day's sport when, in 1978, the Dutch artist was a guest of His Royal Highness The Duke of Edinburgh at a shoot.

Background: sketch from a series, 'A Day's Shooting at Sandringham' by Rien Poortvliet, 1978

Ten of a row of seventeen Purdey shotguns, part of a well used collection of arms which includes a silver Holland revolver and a pair of Purdey pistols

29

BALLROOM CORRIDOR

When it was decided to open Sandringham House to the public, the pictures and artifacts to be displayed in the ballroom corridor were selected especially for their association with King Edward VII and Queen Alexandra. The corridor houses a collection of bronze sculptures and paintings whose subjects encompass abiding interests of the Royal family: sport, horses and the sea.

*The Princes
by Count Gleichen 1878*

*Prince Albert Victor, the Duke of Clarence an
Prince George, later King George V, in
midshipman's uniform by Carl Sohn, 1882*

HRH The Prince Philip
A K Lawrence

HM
Queen Elizabeth II
Sir James Gunn

Princes Albert Victor (Eddy) and George, who entered the Royal Navy at thirteen and twelve years respectively, appear in uniform in a sculpture by Count Gleichen and a painting by Sohn. The frame of the latter is decorated with rope and anchors to add to the nautical flavour. Prince Edward is portrayed as a sportsman and rider, again both in bronze and in oils. His racing yacht, Britannia, is shown in full sail.

Rheumatic fever left Princess Alexandra with a limp, a disability she overcame by having special saddles made and learning again to ride; the painting of her in front of Sandringham House, riding side saddle and accompanied by her dogs, shows her seated the opposite way to normal.

Bookcases along the corridor house part of the Mitchell Collection, an eclectic collection of approximately sixteen hundred volumes bequeathed by George Mitchell to Princess Alexandra in 1878.

The sketches of Her Majesty The Queen and His Royal Highness The Duke of Edinburgh which flank the doors to the ballroom are the most recent Royal portraits to be found at Sandringham.

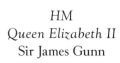

THE BALLROOM

Construction of the ballroom wing was completed in 1883. Princess Alexandra's journal records: 'Our new ball room is beautiful I think and a great success and avoids pulling the hall to pieces each time there is a ball or anything'.

Sixty three feet long, thirty feet wide and twenty three feet high, with a barrelled ceiling for the very best acoustics, the ballroom was suitable for the level of entertaining expected of the heir to the throne. The three magnificent Venetian crystal chandeliers once hung in Buckingham Palace.

On the walls hang oriental arms from The Prince of Wales' tour of India and the Far East. They were brought to Sandringham in 1881 after being exhibited first around Britain and in Paris. The eastern theme continues in the Japanese bronze lamps, Chinese *famille rose* vases and the delicate porcelain and hardwood screen.

In the window alcove are three flags given by Princess Alexandra to two of the world's greatest explorers early in the twentieth century.

The marble bust of Queen Victoria was presented to Prince Edward in 1889, her only official visit to Sandringham

The minstrels' gallery now houses a film projection unit. In addition to occasional use as a cinema, the ballroom is used today for cocktail parties for Estate employees, pensioners and local people.

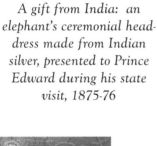

A gift from India: an elephant's ceremonial head-dress made from Indian silver, presented to Prince Edward during his state visit, 1875-76

The cinema projection unit on the minstrels' gallery with comfortable chairs for guests below

The flag given to Shackleton en route to the South Pole

The gift to Captain Scott which he set at the North Pole, later returned to Queen Alexandra by his widow

The second gift to Shackleton on the 'Endurance', 1914

C'91

The Prince was first encouraged to paint as a child and took up watercolour in his early twenties. 'I'd tried to paint when I was about seven or eight when my father had shown me how to do it with oils,' Prince Charles has said. 'Then . . . I suddenly had a yearning to try with watercolours – firstly because it was something different and, secondly, because I thought it was somehow more expressive than oils and such painting was more alive and had more texture and depth than a photograph'.

His Royal Highness The Prince of Wales'
private hobby of painting first became public
in 1987 when one of his watercolours was
selected for display at the annual Royal Academy
summer exhibition. The painting was submitted
under a pseudonym (A G Carrick) and depicted a
Norfolk farm scene.

Sir Hugh Casson, former President of the Royal
Academy, is one of the many British artists to
encourage The Prince of Wales: "He draws
inspiration from ordinary scenes and simple places
that he knows and loves and, like every serious
artist, he paints not just what he sees but what he
is . . . a man happiest in the open air".

His Royal Highness has written of his painting: "It
has revolutionised my life and through the
requirement of intense concentration, it is one of
the most relaxing and therapeutic exercises I
know . . . When I am feeling decidedly gloomy
and claustrophobic in London, it reminds me
where my heart is".

HRH The Prince of Wales painting in Wales, 1994
Photograph: Lesley Donald

Sandringham House
HRH The Prince of Wales
© A G Carrick 1991

THE MUSEUM

The coach houses and stable block which house the museum have had several uses over the last century: the Sandringham Fire Brigade was based here in the 1930s; some of the rooms were used at one time as a police post; and the carving school occupied part of the building from Queen Mary's day until 1957. Today, the Royal garage area, which buzzes with activity when the House is occupied, forms part of the museum, providing a simple but authentic backdrop for vehicles on display.

In 1995 when the museum was being refurbished, an old cupboard was opened for the first time in more than fifty years to reveal two messages written in pencil: "Museum September 20th 1928 Made from

stables, stalls and carriage houses" and "Museum open to the public 1930, July 2nd, at 3d a head. This lasted for five years". The early museum was created by King George V to bring together big game trophies from all of the Royal residences. In 1977, when Sandringham House was opened to the public, pieces commissioned for the Royal family in the last century, commemorative china and some of the gifts presented to Her Majesty The Queen during her reign were brought to the museum for exhibition.

On parade outside the coach house: the Sandringham Fire Brigade, founded by Prince Edward in 1865

In 1900 when King Edward VII purchased a six horsepower Daimler Phaeton he became the first British monarch to own and drive a motor car.

In 1900 Country Gentleman magazine made a motoring prediction: 'Now that the Prince has become a chauffeur, society may be trusted to follow his lead'

In 1977 the motor museum at Beaulieu made a contribution to Jubilee Year and restored the first Royal car to perfect working order

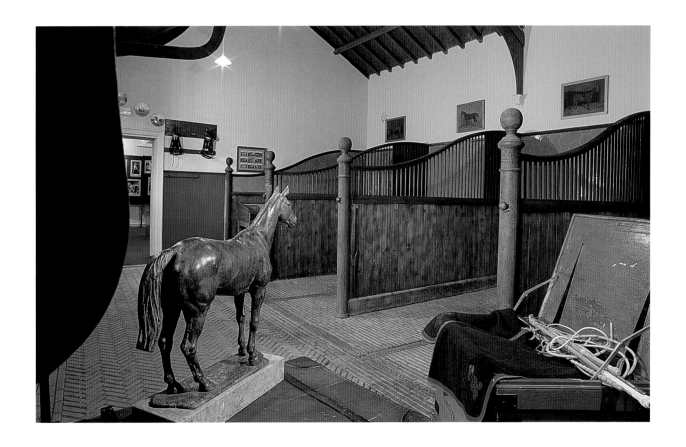

Still in running order, the Phaeton is the highlight of a collection of vehicles owned and used by the Royal family. The miniature Aston Martin is a perfect copy of the famous sports car used by James Bond.

The popularity of motoring as an everyday mode of transport did not diminish the Royal family's love of horses for recreation. A stable, complete with original fittings from the 1870s, was restored in 1995 and now forms part of the museum complex, housing items of saddlery and memorabilia of a rich heritage of horse racing, the sport of kings.

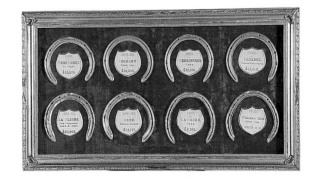

Racing plates: a gift from Prince Edward's greatest trainer, John Porter of Kingsclere

An unusual water carrier in the style of a garden watering can

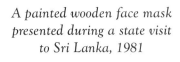

A painted wooden face mask presented during a state visit to Sri Lanka, 1981

'God Save the King' - Prince Edward becomes King Edward VII on coronation, 1902

In the long gallery the wall panels feature a pictorial history of all four monarchs who made Sandringham their private home

Miniature Aston Martin made for HRH The Duke of York in 1966

A series of sepia photographs follows the history of Sandringham's Royal ownership, giving a fascinating insight into life on the Estate.

Three magnificent religious paintings by Sir Noel Paton, commissioned by Queen Victoria for her private chapel at Osborne House, hang in one room. The triptych was given by King George V and Queen Mary to St Mary's Anmer, but conditions within the church were not ideal and, eventually, the paintings began to deteriorate. In 1985 Her Majesty The Queen arranged for them to be restored by the Royal Collection and, when restoration works were completed in 1995, a decision was taken to display the paintings in the museum until St Mary's can take them back.

In common with many estates, Sandringham in the 1870s had a model dairy to provide milk, cream and butter for the House. The dairy was also a charming place for Princess Alexandra to take guests for tea. Styled like a Swiss cottage, it was decorated inside with fine hand-painted Minton tiles. The dairy was demolished in the 1960s but many examples of Minton majolica and tile friezes survive.

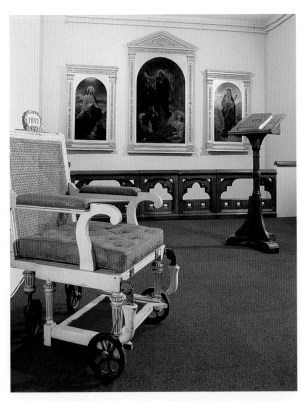

In the triptych room Queen Victoria's wheelchair (1897) is placed alongside the three religious paintings commissioned for her private chapel

Only hand tools were allowed in Her Majesty's Carving School

A delicate pottery corner bracket: a swallow feeds her young

Minton circular plaque: a nymph and child on a lily pond, 1878

Princess Alexandra established at Sandringham schools where the children of Estate workers could learn needlework and woodwork. Under the auspices of Queen Mary, the carving school achieved national acclaim. Its high quality woodwork was exhibited regularly at the Ideal Home Exhibition and was sold from both Sandringham and fine London department stores.

A Minton figure: one of many that decorated the model dairy at Sandringham. The dairy was used for afternoon tea by Queen Alexandra and Queen Mary

Minton majolica fish in a basket: formerly in the dairy

Presented on a visit to Mauritius: Lord Nelson's flagship 'Victory'

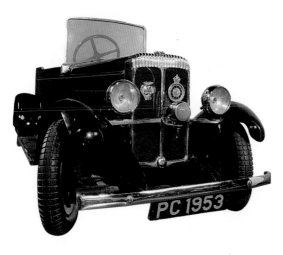

From the miniature 1930s Daimler (top left), enjoyed by HM The Queen and HRH The Princess Margaret, to the vast splendour of the 1954 Rolls Royce Phantom (top right), all of the vehicles were well used before retiring to the museum. The Daimler shooting brakes (lower left) carried family and guests over the Estate and the vast grouse moors of Balmoral. In 1961, HRH The Duke of Edinburgh's personal specifications – a five speed gear box and leather finish – were incorporated into the Alvis TD21 drop head coupé (lower right).

The administration of a 20,000 acre estate with diverse interests is a complex business. The Estate Office, located in York Cottage, is not open to the public, but ledgers and maps from the archives and antiquated office equipment have been assembled to demonstrate how office technology and practices have changed over the years. The 19th century letter copying machine was first used at Buckingham Palace over a century ago.

'Foster's Improved Fire Engine' - the pump which handled the Sandringham House fire of 1891

The collection of big game trophies

In 1865 Prince Edward founded the Sandringham Fire Brigade. Manned by volunteer Estate workers, it was equipped with the latest fire fighting equipment. In 1891 and again in 1903 the brigade saved the House from serious fire damage, and, during the second world war, took the Merryweather Fire Engine to Norwich to fight fires caused by German bombing. In 1968, after more than a hundred years of duty, the Sandringham Fire Brigade was amalgamated into the Norfolk Fire Service, but a tradition remains and a number of Estate workers continue to be employed as auxiliary firemen, supporting the local fire service in emergencies.

The rooms in which King George V gathered big game trophies are still in use. Part of Sandringham's history, the trophies are displayed today with great sensitivity and innovation. The first room, styled as a Victorian baronial hall, displays European and American animals. The second takes visitors to the jungles and plains of Africa and Asia, attempting, with artistic licence, to show how native species live and survive today.

The 1939 Merryweather Fire Engine: called to the bombing of the city of Norwich in World War II

41

THE CHURCH

The Church of St Mary Magdalene, considered to be the finest carrstone building in existence

Sir Alfred Gilbert's memorial to the Duke of Clarence: St George, in aluminium inset with ivory

Sandringham's association with the church of St Mary Magdalene dates back to the sixteenth century when the present church was entirely rebuilt by William Cobbes. Two hundred years later and only six years before the Estate was purchased for Prince Albert, the building was extensively restored by Lady Harriet Cowper.

Links between church and the Estate have grown from strength to strength and St Mary's, a country church of exceptional historic interest, has become a public place of private worship.

The Royal family at Sandringham, Christmas 1994

Photograph courtesy of Eastern Daily Press

42

SANDRINGHAM AND THE VISITOR

Facilities for visitors have been much improved since 1977 when Sandringham House was first opened to the public.

A tractor and trailer tour, introduced in 1992, offers visitors a tour of the country park with an interesting commentary by the driver, and in 1995 a land train was provided to transport less mobile visitors through the grounds to the House.

The new visitor centre, opened in 1994, offers an air conditioned self service restaurant, a tea room, ice cream kiosk and plant centre where visitors can purchase herbs, flowers and plants nurtured on the Estate. The well stocked gift shop is a delight in itself offering a host of beautiful items from the very small to the very special – truly something for everyone.

Photograph: Farrows

Restaurant (above)

Gift Shop (right)

Tractor Tour (left)

Visitor Centre (below)

Photograph: Farrows

WILDLIFE SKETCHBOOK

Other parts of Norfolk cannot quite compare with Sandringham for scenic variety. The churchyard of St Mary Magdalene overlooks undulating parkland and rolling woodland; a hundred years ago much of this was open heath and scrubland.

Nearby, six hundred acres of woodland have been opened to the public as a country park. This area stems from the nineteenth century requirement for timber which resulted in extensive woodland planting. The great variety of trees is due in part to the travels of successive generations of the Royal family who brought back from abroad many exotic species. Now established woodland areas provide shelter and nourishment for a wide variety of wildlife as well as a renewable timber resource.

The enhancement of natural history and encouragement of wildlife has always been a priority at Sandringham. Part of the Estate lies within a region designated an 'Area of Outstanding Natural Beauty', within which a 'Site of Special Scientific Interest' is managed by English Nature as a national nature reserve and Ramsar site (European Community designated wildlife area).

Over a hundred species of fungi can be found on the Estate, ranging from the penny bun (*bolectus edultis*), which is edible, to the highly poisonous but beautiful fly agaric (*amenita muscaria*).

Almost a hundred species of bird can be found, from the jay, one of Britain's most wary birds, to rare hawks, such as marsh and Montague harriers. Wild pheasants breed and thrive all over the Estate.

Not only the vegetation changes with the seasons, the green woodpecker is a permanent inhabitant but the great grey shrike and other migratory birds return to Sandringham each winter. Mallards, mandarin ducks and snow geese, which use this area of East Anglia as a breeding ground, are frequent visitors to the lakes at Sandringham.

Two nature trails have been established within the country park for walkers: the blue trail is one mile and the yellow trail two and a quarter miles long. For the motorist, the scenic drive offers secluded parking and picnic sites, and, for those who prefer a conducted tour, the tractor and trailer driver identifies many of the rarities to be found in the beautiful environs of Sandringham.

SANDRINGHAM IN WINTER

Although the grounds are glorious in summer, the winter months have always been special at Sandringham.

Throughout his reign, King Edward VII's 'official' birthday was celebrated in the summer, but he always celebrated the day on which he was born, 9th November, at 'The Big House'. Similarly, Queen Alexandra's birthday on 1st December was celebrated here among the short, sharp frosts of winter.

In the early years of Her Majesty's reign, the Royal family continued the tradition set by King Edward VII and gathered together at Sandringham for Christmas, but by 1964 the family had grown and the festivities transferred to Windsor Castle with its greater space. In 1989, however, tradition was restored and since then the Royal family have celebrated both Christmas and New Year here in the safe seclusion of the English winter.

A winter visitor: the woodcock

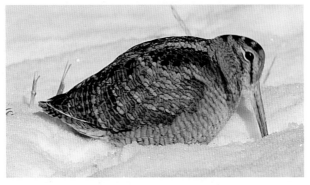

*Main picture: Queen Alexandra's Nest
on the edge of the Upper Lake*

THE ESTATE AND ROYAL STUD

Prince Edward's acquisition in 1862 of 7,000 acres was, at the time, considered insufficient to support Sandringham House. Since then, the Estate has been expanded to over 20,000 acres, including villages, heath, woodland and farmland.

In addition to the country park, around 200 acres of land adjacent to the grounds is managed as a private park. Here, trees have been planted to emphasise the higher ground and to frame the view between Sandringham and West Newton churches. The park is now used for a number of special events, including the annual flower show and the carriage driving event and country show which were initiated in 1983 by His Royal Highness The Duke of Edinburgh.

Farmland accounts for 16,000 acres. Approximately two-thirds is farmed by tenants and 200 acres are devoted to the production of apples and soft fruit. Many people flock to Sandringham each year to pick their own strawberries, raspberries and apples which can also be purchased in season from the visitor centre.

Timber and timber products are sold from the sawmill. Forestry operations continue to shape the local landscape which requires careful long term planning. Ecological issues are always important at Sandringham with careful consideration given to the requirements of game and to wildlife conservation generally.

The monumental bronze statue of Persimmon situated outside the Royal Stud

In 1886, Prince Edward established two stud farms on the Estate, one at Sandringham and one at Wolferton, and very soon the Royal Stud became one of England's most influential. The brood mare Perdita II produced two of racing's legends: Persimmon, who won the St Leger and the Derby in 1896 and Diamond Jubilee who won the 1900 Triple Crown. Prince Edward ploughed the prize money, millions of pounds in today's terms, into the Estate, particularly the vast walled gardens. When his guests expressed amazement at the acres of kitchen garden, herbaceous borders, ornamental pergolas and greenhouses full of exotic fruit, he replied simply: "All Persimmon, all Persimmon".

Written by HRH The Duke of Edinburgh and Gill Pattinson with additional contributions by Peter Morgan and John Martin Robinson.

Edited by Sue Baker. Photography by Peter Smith of Newbery Smith. Map and Wildlife Sketchbook by Nick McCann.

Additional photography: Grounds – Brian Chapple; HM The Queen – Richard Tilbrook; Wildlife – Roger Tidman; Archive photographs – The Royal Collection; A J Humbert's drawings of Sandringham House courtesy of the RIBA; Memorial to the Duke of Clarence – Pitkin Pictorials; Persimmon – Ann Clifton.

Earlier books, guidebooks and magazine articles have been researched in the production of this guide and acknowledgements are due to: Macmillan Press *The Royal Encyclopedia* 1991; Sir Harold Nicolson *King George VI* 1952; George Plumptre *Edward VII* 1995; Little Brown & Co *HRH The Prince of Wales' Watercolours* 1991.

Designed and published by English Life Publications Ltd and printed in Great Britain.